K105

P9-CSV-962

GIRLS
A to Z

by Eve Bunting

Illustrated by Suzanne Bloom

Boyds Mills Press

To all our wonderful girls:
Chris, Debbie, Tracy, Dana, Anna, Tory, and Erin
—E. B.

To my girlfriends who all work hard to help make dreams
come true.
—S. B.

Text copyright © 2002 by Eve Bunting
Illustrations copyright © 2002 by Suzanne Bloom
All rights reserved

Published by Boyds Mills Press, Inc.
A Highlights Company
815 Church Street
Honesdale, Pennsylvania 18431
Printed in China
Visit our Web site at www.boydsmillspress.com

Publisher Cataloging-in-Publication Data (U.S.)

Bunting, Eve.
   Girls : a to z / by Eve Bunting ; illustrated by Suzanne Bloom.—1st ed.
[32] p. : col. ill. ;   cm.
Summary: Girls with names ranging from Aliki to Zoe imagine themselves in various
fun and creative professions.
ISBN 1-56397-147-X
1. Occupations — Juvenile literature. 2. Women — Employment — Juvenile literature.
3. Professions — Juvenile literature. (1. Occupations. 2. Women — Employment.
3. Professions. 4. Alphabet.) I. Bloom, Suzanne. II. Title.
331.7/ 02/ 082 [E] 21   CIP HF5381.2.B86 2002
2001094574

First edition, 2002
The text of this book is set in 24-point Souvenir Medium.

10 9 8 7 6 5

Aliki is an astronaut,

Belinda likes ballet,

Chris is a computer whiz—
she's online every day.

Dana is a dentist,

Eve's an engineer,

Fiona puts out fires,

Gwen's a gondolier.

Haifa likes to stay at home,

Irene makes ice cream,

Kate's a kicker for the team.

Lupe's a librarian,

Maria meditates,

Nicky is a nanny,

Olive operates.

Pat is our next president,

Quinn's the harvest queen,

Rosie races racing cars,

Sal sells gasoline.

Tanya teaches little kids
to say the alphabet,

Ula is an umpire,

Velma is a vet.

Windemere writes picture books,

Xi plays the xylophone,

Yolanda studies yoga,

Zoe's zoo's well known.

Girls,
Be anything you want to be.
Do what you want to do.
Dream any dream you want to dream.
The world is here for you.